Best wishes,
Ellen Argyros

Feta in Brine

by Ellen Argyros

PublishAmerica
Baltimore

First printing

ISBN: 1-60563-374-7
PUBLISHED BY PUBLISHAMERICA, LLLP
www.publishamerica.com
Baltimore

Printed in the United States of America

Dedicated with love to
Dad, Yaya, Uncle Mickey, Bapa, and Gregory,
who left the party too soon,
and to Mom, who stayed behind to help clean up the mess

Table of Contents

Nitroglycerin Tablet, Taken Under the Tongue 7
When Did I First Feel like a Grown-up? 9
Out of the Fangorn into the Xanadu 11
The Castle of Mytilene 14
Danielle, Our Day Lily 16
New Tiles 18
Biology Love Poem 19
Sale 20
Elegy for Cora Jones 23
Watching 27
Feta in Brine 29
Yaya's House 31
My One Night Stand with Bill Evans 33
Elegy for Three Silver Maples and a Man 37
Parallel Birthday Party Universes 39
Daddy Longlegs 41
Centipede Morning 46
Parable of the Vomiting Friend 48
Scene from My Window 53
A Small Holocaust 55
Elegy for Aunt Cleo 57
Origins 58
Anne of Cleves 60
Elegy for Margaret Newlin 62
Onion Soup 66
Kindred Spirits 68
Seized by Love 72
Dadscapes 74
Bratty Little Sister 76
Secret Agent 77

The Wanted Child 79
While Reading on the Cell Cycle, I Find a Poem 81
The Dragonfly 82
Moth at 5 a.m. 84
Millipede 86
Graveyard 88
The Red Efts of Ganoga Lake 89
Old Haunts 90
He's Got Mail 93
Darfur Lullaby 94
Gesture Drawing 95
Memory of a Texture 97
Cold Potato Boy 99
Greece with Kids 101
Portrait of Uncle Mickey 103
Stranger at the Door 105
Baby College 109

Nitroglycerin Tablet, Taken Under the Tongue

My father was the soft smell of baby powder.
He was the clink of billiard balls in the basement,
bent across the green, frowning and strategizing his next three shots.
He was a smooth and effortless stroke,
and he was a lesson scrawled in blue chalk on the basement wall:
"Never hit the cue ball in anger—the cue ball will only do what you taught it."

He was often a pack of cigarettes,
often a hangover.

He was a denim jacket with matching jeans.
He was a grocery store trip to Grand Union with Yaya, every Sunday after church.

He was Badri the Bandit
and Bernard Mergendeiler
and Tony Kirby, and
he couldn't take it with him

because he was also a set of clogged arteries,
a heart condition
from a long family history of heart conditions…
angina, pulmonary embolisms, calcified aortic valves.
He should have been a triple bypass at Deborah Hospital in 1970,
    when such operations were still experimental.
Instead, he was dilatory,
a vasodilator, to be exact,
a nitroglycerin tablet every few hours, taken under the tongue.

And then one day, in the strangest of alchemies, he was suddenly cold and made of wax,
a handsome black suit
at the Francioni, Taylor, and Lopez funeral home.
He was still enough that I could borrow a scissors from Mr. Lopez to cut off a lock of his silky black hair.

He was, and still is, pages of signatures in the memorial book—
Gregory Nicolas, Charlie Evans, Marty Maloney,
many of them long since gone,
selfishly taking their memories of him with them, like stolen seashells.

He had once been a warm lap,
a smell of English Leather and sweat and cigarettes,
a bedtime story about a tiny girl called Eggen who lived in people's ears and ate earwax.
He had once been an extravagant papier-mache frog and
a tuna fish salad with potato chips
(When I wanted him to make it, I would leave the ingredients on the front step and then ring the doorbell.)

And in a book about the moon that I lost years ago,
he was a message on the frontispiece:
"To Ellen the moon-lover, from Dad the Ellen-lover"

When Did I First Feel like a Grown-up?

Not upon graduating from college,
for that was a time of Honors Exams,
External Examiners, signifiers and signifieds,
Derrida and Lacan and Cixous…
Suddenly I was marching in lock-step while
trying to balance a mortarboard
without bobby pins.
And this one was going to grad school and that one law school
and I didn't know quite what I'd be doing next.

Not upon getting married,
for that was a time of seed pearls
and spaghetti straps
and mermaid gowns with draped busts
and Chicken Kiev and carrot layer cake
and the calculus of seating arrangements
and negotiating the mine field of injured feelings
and wondering what one's cousin
might possibly be saying to make one's old roommate so red,
and the reception was fun, but I was tired and just
wanted to drive off with Ken and say,
"Hi Husband" to try on for size the strange new word
that fit even more awkwardly than my wedding dress.

Not upon teaching for the first time
for that was a time when all my signifiers and signifieds
could not prepare me for the student who declared
that Frank O'Conner had committed
plagiarism in "My Oedipus Complex"
"because, after all, Freud invented the Oedipus Complex"

and me gaping with awe at my student's ignorance
as well as my own, and trying to stumble my way through an explanation
about the difference between an allusion and plagiarism.

Not even upon giving birth for the first time
for that was a time of water breaking and counting contractions
and pitocin drips and breathing exercises and epidurals
and dilating cervixes and the cutting of the cord
and the colostrum and the meconium and cord care and nursing non-stop
and my feeling that that hospital staff was committing
some sort of dreadful error in entrusting this fragile creature to my
bumbling care and wondering how Ken could so calmly
thread those rubbery little arms through that tiny kimono shirt.

No, it wasn't until my oldest son came home
from kindergarten with his first permission slip
that I felt like an adult.
Unpacking his Power Rangers back-pack,
I found the yellow sheet.
A field trip to Jacob's, the corner store,
to see how hotdogs were made.
I circled "Parent," then signed my name.
"This is it," I thought. "Now I am an adult."

Out of the Fangorn into the Xanadu

Old Treebeard the Ent
was gnarled and bent
and hopelessly on in years.
The Third Age had gone.
The Fourth had moved on,
and still he retained his fears

that those making him yearn
would never return
but had found a happier place
where the soil was black
and soft and rich
and sweet breezes kissed one's face.

Since the Entwives had left,
his heart was bereft
of their laughter and leaves and song.
They'd found a new place
leaving nary a trace
of where they did now belong.

He went on a quest
through the land he loved best
over rock and stream and dale.
He asked every bird
if it had heard,
and he plodded through storm and gale.

He asked every bird
if it had heard
of where the Entwives went.
But none of them knew
so away they flew.
Sad root-steps homeward bent.

Only one aged crow
purported to know
where the Entwives had made their home.
It was far away from Treebeard
near a stately pleasure dome.
Fair Xanadu, under skies so blue,
is what they now called home.

The Entwives wore no girdles now
their roots sprawled where they wished
near Alph, the sacred river, where the
Entwives often fished
with many an incense-bearing tree.
But were they really free?

They'd jumped the pages of Treebeard's book
straight into Xanadu.
They never looked back at their former lives
or doubted what they'd do
"No Ents for us, with all their needs!
No Entlings underfoot!
By root and twig, who gives a fig
Where the frying pan's been put?!
We're sick of serving as nursemaids
We want to have our fun," they cried,

but they knew they'd lied, for their sea
was without sun.

And the walls and towers were girdled round
and the forests, old as the hills,
like Fangorn (which they thought they'd left
for newer thrills and chills).
And that damsel with the dulcimer
proved nothing but a pest:
She played all night 'neath the waning light
and disturbed the Entwives' rest.

So Treebeard longed in solitude
while the Entwives covered their ears
and shouted, *"Damn you, damsel!"*
and other nasty jeers.
Sometimes the Entwives missed the Ents
and yearned for the forest they knew,
but it's hard to return to Fangorn
when you've been to Xanadu.

The Castle of Mytilene

The blind woman in me who visited
the remains of the castle at Mytilene
was overwhelmed by the pine—
the soft pine needles underfoot,
the cooling shade of the towering pines,
and the soft resin-scented air.

The deaf woman in me
smiled at the old ticket taker,
who sat at a makeshift
rickety folding poker table
with a plastic jug of iced tea
next to her portable radio.

The ruined walls of the castle
outline the footprint
of the structure.
The roof is gone,
the sense of enclosure, gone.
All is exposed.

Only the sun everywhere,
and the scent of pine,
and the blue Aegean below
just visible through the crumbling arch
through which one spies
a road with three passersby.
You wave in English.
She waves back in Greek.

The mute woman in me
wants to cry out,
"Why didn't I bring my camera?"

No gift shop, no postcards, only
memory, faulty and partial,
underexposed
out of focus
fading and
rife with
pine

Danielle, Our Day Lily

"Lay her i' the earth,
And from her fair and unpolluted flesh
May violets spring…"
Hamlet, V, i, 227-229

When I heard the news,
I shook my head.
The only thing to do was to plant my seven day lilies.

The first is for that long-awaited baby girl, sucking her fist in the crib, pounced on by fond brothers.
The second, for the toddler in a floral swimsuit, one cheek hanging out as she hopped in shallow waves.
The third for the small girl, seized by a large dog, rescued by her mother.
The fourth for the chic young woman I knew, with cropped red hair, the film student in Boston.
The fifth is for her hopes and aspirations, the Spike Lee films, the chance at this or that.
The sixth is for the shards and flints she suffered.
The seventh is for her mother, needing sedation to cope with her pain, her father staring out at the night, her three brothers who will never be the same.

I spread the peat moss,
space the plants,
carefully dig the holes,
water each ball of roots,
set the root ball in its hole,
pat the dirt,
and water it again.

Your body, shipped east,
is a cold and lonely bulb.
Your mother will know what to do with it.
She will receive it with grace, as she always has.
She will take up her gardener's tools,
    her shovel, her trowel, her spade.
She will dig a hole
in the center of her chest,
line it with photographs of birthday parties, recitals, graduations,
soften it with lullabies,
water it with hot tears,
and take you back.
She will carry you now,
    as she did long ago,
but this time she will never set you down
but wait
    with a mother's patience
for you to bloom

    a bright and pale orange flower

again and again and again

In memory of Danielle Surrette

New Tiles

Slather paste over the grimy yellow linoleum,
its ripped seams, its yesterday pattern,
slather it in ridged rows which paste over the insult
(like a criminal drowned beneath the waves).

The wretched mod linoleum
has become
    just another layer
 in the archaeology of my kitchen.

Hammer down grey underbacking,
large flat sheets of it—
already an improvement.

Next, lay the rigid geometry of the tiles:

cold	white	hard	clean	pure
truth	honor	art	God	quiet
sharp	order	peace	good	bright

Thegroutconcealsthegrid.

If	only	the	world	could	be
so	pure	and	good	and	new…

            Weapons inspectors spend sleepless nights
            while soldiers gird for war.

Biology Love Poem

She'll be his sucrase,
he'll be her sucrose.
She'll lie like an enzyme in a textbook illustration,
active site, hollowed out in the shape of
an inverted triangle.
He, her substrate, will quietly hover above her,
inverted triangle poised—
prepared for a perfect fit
(or an induced fit, if she's not quite in the mood).
Then they will form their
substrate-enzyme complex,
after which she will gently break him down
into his component parts,
sigh at the loss of him.

It's the perfect night for a coupling:
the perfect temperature:
    hot, but not too hot.
the perfect pH:
    not too acidic, nor too base.

Sale

First of all, what to call it.
Rummage, yard, garage, or moving.
The action, the place, or the reason why.
It's a moving sale all right.
We are moving.
We want the objects to move.
And I am dislocated at every purchase,
every transaction, every foreclosing of possibility, every setting adrift of a memory, every translation of memory into commodity, of commodity into vacancy.

Every object is priced to go, except for my son's Gameboy cartridge, which he has stubbornly priced at $20.

Secondly, what to put in it.
Outgrown toys, dusty inhabitants of the basement, old wedding presents, never used.
One single silver candlestick holder, wrapped in plastic, missing its mate.
An electric clock with "To have and to hold, for richer, for poorer, til death do us part, Kenneth and Ellen, June 17, 1989" written on it. The tyranny of personalized gifts.
The Salad Shooter, a device for shredding lettuce. Still in the box. (I *like* to tear up the romaine…)
The four Kenneth chairs—how could I resist them? named after you—purchased at the Door Store in Cambridge, used for two decades, the cheapest we could find, $26 apiece. A woman and her husband drive up in a mini-van. "Make me an offer," I tell her. "A buck apiece?" "Sold."

My oldest son—wanting to please his "toss everything" dad—places his clay model of the Parthenon out on the small plastic table he and his friend Mitchell had found the week before.
It sits there. Stoical. Proud.
It attracts the attention of his friend, Adam, who pays the 50 cents for it, thinking he will use it with his Lego men.
I feel comforted by the thought that Zach's Parthenon
is in friendly hands.

The large plastic orangeyellowbluegreen climbing toy. Little Tykes. We paid $150 for it and owned it for a decade. When the boys were little, we had it set up in our dining room in lieu of a dining set. I could look over at them as they crawled up the slide barefoot (for traction), made their way to the top, and waved triumphantly at me. Then, as they got older and we began to reclaim our home, we demoted it to a place beneath the apple tree. It provided access to the crook of the tree. Its nooks full of cobwebs and spider eggs, it has not been touched for a while.

Ken had written "$25" on a piece of masking tape and placed it on the thing. "Is $20 too low?" a portly woman asked, her teenage and toddler boys accompanying her. "No, that's fine." She writes a check. My husband finds a mallet, and we disassemble it. The teenage son patiently waits for me to sponge off each newly exposed cruddy area, then packs the pieces of the thing in their van. The woman is smiling at her good deal

but the space beneath the apple tree now looks newly erased,
like a child's drawing with a hole in it.

Who will keep vigil with me during this day of loss and gain?
Neighbors.

Connie, whose husband and son are on a Boy Scouts trip, sits on the stoop with me, chatting all day.
Jackie, teenager who lost her father last year.
Her mother Bonnie, widow and mother of eight, stops by for a bit.
Shannon, five year old girl. Left to roam for hours each day.
Grubby, needy, slow to speak, barefoot, Shannon haunts the sale all day. Fingering this. Climbing into that.

They want to be neighborly.
They understand loss.
Shannon lovingly handles every McDonald's Happy Meal toy in the bucket
    as if to console it for being unwanted.

Elegy for Cora Jones

I.
The hunter who found your corpse
will never be the same.

The coroner who probed
the eight jagged stab wounds,
delicately measuring the depth,
the angle of insertion,
tried hard not to think of his own Jess,
straight brown hair and scabby knees
like yours.
He will never be the same.

And I, replaying a rescue—
car pulling up to the girl on the bicycle
me yelling "HEY YOU!"
and the car screeching off—
I will never be the same.

II.
The corpse gives off
the sickly sweet smell of blue
berry bagels.

It is not you.

The difference between you and it, Cora,
is the difference between your grandma's backyard
(rusty swingset, apple tree in bloom, wet swimsuits hung on the line)
and the surface of the moon—

icy vacant airless rock
cratered like his face.

It is not you.

III.
(Three twigs and a squirrel bear witness.
The swift movement, the cries startle the squirrel.)

My warmest flannel jacket, the ammunition, the patch from the DNR, the camouflage stuff, Jack's two-gallon thermos filled with coffee, the gun newly oiled, the target re-attached, Emma's roast beef sandwiches on rye, two bags of apples, the decoy…

He thinks he forgot nothing.
What he forgot was how to prepare for what he would find in the woods—the body a salami cut open here and here, the clotted blood, the tangled hair, the fear frozen in her eyes.

Behave with utmost gallantry.
First remove the curious
daddy long leg from her cheek.
(She might have shrieked to see it.)
Then brush the dirt
from her lips.
Cover her nakedness
with your jacket.

The coroner sighs and reaches for an even smaller scalpel. He records the angle of insertion in his report. He turns up the volume of the radio.

IV.
There was a girl.

She had a crush on a boy with green eyes in Phys. Ed.
She spoke for two hours on the phone each night with Cathy about this boy and that boy and chemistry
homework and Mr. Mertikas and auditions and when was the *Jane Eyre* paper due and how many pages did it have to be and how many ads did you sell for yearbook and on and on until her pa yelled at her to "Get off the phone, grandma might be trying to call, and here you are tying up the lines…"
She stood before a mirror in her first real bra, admiring
her silhouette ("Where'd you get them teeny raisins?" Aunt Rita teased.)
She lived for chats with Cathy, chocolate licorice, knock knock jokes, *The Babysitters Club.*
She was learning to ride with no hands.

V.
The hunter has no heart
for deer
and will not touch
his gun.

The coroner cannot sow radishes
or hear "My Brown-Eyed Girl"
on the radio
without sobbing.

I spend hours rescuing you
over and over
after the deed is done.

Know, child, that for every menacing presence
lurking by the roadside
there is a dark-eyed hunter,
a gentle coroner,
and me, the sometime poet,
trying to animate the dead
trying to comfort the living

stealing into my sons' rooms,
jealously watching them sleep,
watching their small chests
rise and fall.

Watching

for Aunt Andrea

There is the question of these new ones.
The rules are firm.
You can only watch.

The boy has curly hair. Naked, just after his bath, he is so Cupid-like you expect wings
for shoulder blades.
He is intent on one matchbox car, carefully driven along a narrow floorboard.
The occasional suck at his juicebox.

You knew him when he was just a fat lady.

Once you watched his fever spike to 105, the fretful crying, the panicked parents, the busy signal, the phone slammed down, the midnight trip to the one 24 hour pharmacy twelve miles away…

To touch his burning brow, you would happily toss Mytilene into the sea.

The girl is fat. Her feet are fat. In her daisy sundress, her diaper is fat. She smiles with her tongue. You watch her bite your daughter's nipple, defy every "No!", take all the pots back out, knock over the trash, dance in the kitty litter, and drop her zwieback on the floor seven times in a row.

Her mother inhales deeply and presses a frowning brow against the cool windowpane.

You extend your hand. It passes through one willful toddler, one angry mother, and a kitchen table wet with spilled milk.

The rules are clear. No touching, comforting, singing, scolding, straightening, putting away, rocking, cooking—no making your presence felt. No fresh-baked koularakia and milk. No "Efhoreesto, Yaya!"

It is purgatory,
this silent witnessing.

It's hardest when they're sick, mischievous, tasting something new, about to grab that hot pan, frightened, falling off to sleep, freshly clean, dressed up, straining to make a kaka, coloring, building, dancing, looking at a book,

on the verge of something
cute or dangerous.

Could Dante have imagined
a more effective punishment?

silent witness
yearning eyes
unrequited grandma sighs

Feta in Brine

I comforted Yaya twice,
after men she loved had died.
After Papou's death,
she babysat me.
I, a newborn, needing
to be rocked and held and fed
and diapered and given mustard plasters
and enemas.
Then, fifteen years later,
after her boys were in the ground,
I would sit with her.
She would tell me stories
of growing up in Mytilene.

Yaya and I had visited
Mytilene when I was twelve.
I remember sitting with her and her sisters,
all of them bursting into peals of laughter,
sparking my greekless curiosity.
"What did she say?" I would beg.
"Lairn Grik!" she would scold.

On Saturday nights I would be sent to spend the night with Yaya.
I'd sleep on a cot
under green wool
blankets—hunter's green and smelling of mothballs—
and in the morning she would prepare the incense
and walk solemnly through her apartment
making the sweet sad smoke
and chanting, *"Ayos ethos, Ayos ethos, Ayos elanamos, Elais animus…"*

We would stop at her altar
where she would pray.
Panagia, the Virgin Mary, had brought her twenty-two year old
son home
from Korea, unscathed.

Yaya liked to cook
lamb with new potatoes,
kiefthedes, hamburger and macaroni,
avgolemeno soup.

In Yaya's fridge, there was a plastic pitcher with
blocks of feta
floating in brine.
There was the inevitable lemon.
And in her pantry,
jars of calamata olives,
boxes of Orzo pasta,

Not much to snack on
at Yaya's.
Raw ingredients
made palatable
only by her.

Yaya's House

Time, in amber, took a well-deserved nap at Yaya's house.
You could watch the dust floating in a sunbeam.

Yaya had no toys in her apartment,
no books, nothing designed for children.
Only one Greek magazine from 1956.
She watched *Days of Our Lives, The Doctors, As the World Turns.*

I learned to play with dust motes,
greeting cards, dead leaves.

I climbed under coffee tables,
found domestic bliss in a hedge,
discovered a suburb in the attic
where an old doll and a stuffed dog lay untouched for ages.
In that attic, Maryellen and I
had husbands "in the war"
and our children slept a lot.

Once, Maryellen and I climbed out an attic window onto the roof.
We lay on our stomachs with our faces over the edge
looking down three stories into the alleyway
until Uncle Mickey found us,
wisely telling Yaya
nothing
but quietly nailing that window shut.

The attic stairs were very narrow.
Once, after witnessing Maryellen falling downstairs,
I learned to go down

on my bottom
bump,
          bump,
                    bump.

There was plenty of danger and boredom
at Yaya's house.

My One Night Stand with Bill Evans

Face it, Bill.
We were made for each other.

(A soft drumbeat, please. Something classy. Brushes on the high hat.)

I, looking deadly,
stroll into the nightclub where you are playing,
sit at a table near the piano, listen thoughtfully,
swat away interested men,
then walk up to you, cock my head, and request that you play
"Alice in Wonderland."
Obligingly, you play the pretty waltz, touching
the keys with tantalizing
delicacy, a cigarette dangling
from your lips

During a break, you slouch over to my table, smiling shyly.
You knew I was going to ask for "Alice."
We both love Carroll's bizarre tale, think it
surreal, resonant, disturbing.
You listen well.
You develop my ideas with me.
You gaze directly, your voice intimate.
You ask if you can buy me a drink.
I, in grad school, chat with you about Thomas Hardy.
What we like about Jude.
I am writing my dissertation on George Eliot. You liked *Middlemarch*
but thought Dorothea a bit of a prig.

Our conversation so fluid,
it is soon 3 a.m.
and the waitress is wiping the table.

There would be no sex—not yet, anyway.
I would have to play it cool,
reel you in slowly.
This is, after all, the fifties.
I would show up at your gigs…not all of them
(got to keep you guessing, can't be too predictable).
You would play "Alice in Wonderland"—our song—
with the occasional glance my way,
cigarette still dangling.
I would smile into my Virgin Mary.

Our first weeks would be intoxicating, terrifying, exciting.
Eye contact with you across a crowded, smoky bar
would be far more intense
than the actual body contact afterwards.

But let's face it, gorgeous.
It wouldn't have lasted.
In time, we might have moved in together and played at marriage,
but I would not have been able to tolerate your smoking or your drug habit
or the shady characters it brought you
into contact with.
You were not the jealous type, but I would have been.

There would have been other women—
coffee, creme, and every shade inbetween—
draping themselves across your
piano.

You, consummate improviser, would have occasionally indulged
in a one night stand
because it seemed the thing to do at the time.
There would have been ugly scenes.
A pot thrown at your piano, denting it.
Remorse. Forgiveness. The scene replayed.

Oh, Bill. I've done the best I could.
Married my own beautiful nerd—
who loves your music,
who can play like you—
even play "Alice in Wonderland"—
who enjoys Thomas Hardy.

We have two children, two jobs, two cars, and too little
danger and pain.
He has never
played with Miles, never
had anyone threaten to break his fingers, never
gotten strung out on heroin, never
lived with a black woman for a decade, never
caused a woman to throw herself
under a subway train, never
been Orpheus, with Eurydice safely in Hades…

In our household, Orpheus is
unclogging the upstairs toilet,
while Eurydice is in the kitchen,
loading the dishwasher.

There is, however, a CD player in that kitchen.

Here is my secret—

I listen to *Blue in Green*
while I wash the
dishes.
You play for me
blue in green—that's what I am—
and we are smiling smoky smiles
across the miles

Elegy for Three Silver Maples and a Man

In memory of Richard Much

i.
Three sturdy maple giants
three foot thick around
solid, albeit shady, citizens
standing long before the world wars
century old witnesses

roped down today

first the leafy branches
then the thicker limbs
then the tree itself, roped, cut strategically
pulled into the street

the tree men from Asplundh
Lilliputians scurrying across Gulliver's chest
chainsawing limbs
then the machine with its claw
hauling sections of the great rotten torso
—black and hollow with rot—
hauling it off
to some chipping graveyard,
while greedy light spills into every shadow
of our exposed front yards

ii.
You once peeled the toilet paper off of a cardboard tube
for my sons' gerbil.
Father of eight,

builder of a house up north,
five years of weekends,
sire and sturdy oak.
You also lay low
lie pale on the couch at midday
two houses down.

No teams of tree experts, ropes, chainsaws, cherry picker trucks,
tree chippers, claws
necessary to pull you down

The cancer consumes you with its own grim efficiency
first your leafy branches
then the thicker limbs
then the trunk itself, roped, cut strategically
pulled onto the couch.

Another great one made horizontal.

Small talk flew away with the sparrows,
abandoning their nests.
There is nothing to say but the truth
of love, sorrow, death, and loss.
Those left behind must
sweep away the fallen chips,
find shade in other places.

Parallel Birthday Party Universes

I went to Walgreen's
to pick up a developed set of film.
I was worried because I'd accidentally opened the
back of the camera with the film still in it.
So I wasn't sure what I'd get.

When I opened up the yellow framed envelope
(in the car because I couldn't wait),
there was definitely something weird about the photos.

There were ghosts in the pictures.
Images of old friends—Mitchell, Cody, Corey—
taken from our former life,
in Appleton.
What were they doing there?
Quiet, insistent, they stood
and intruded upon our new reality.

It took a while to realize what I'd done…
…superimposed new images upon
a lost roll of film.

An odd concatenation of past and present.
Will Lowry—new friend, pianist, football player,
lives in a million dollar home—
had a birthday barbecue
with seventeen boys.
In one shot, he's grinning wickedly as he prepares
to spang a water balloon.

Hold the photo to the side, however,
and there is Corey, fatherless and one of eight,
looking off to the side,
Cody and Mitchell.
They're in line at GymKids,
where we had a birthday party for Max.

In another shot, Will's mom Soomi
is making water balloons with Ken.
Her smile the center of the composition.
Tip the photo, and you see Max looking down,
Cody and Evan again, looking off to the side.
Objects of desire always elsewhere.

In another, the basketball upon which
a strange insect had perched
last week
is juxtaposed with Max looking up
and Corey looking out.
Traces of our past
haunt us still,
insert themselves into our days,
say, "No, no, you're not finished with us quite yet."

Daddy Longlegs

There were no little girls
that I knew of
living near me
except for Alberta Vaughters
who lived   way down at the end of the block.
(She might as well have been on the moon.)

Instead, across the street from us lived a family with five boys:
George,
    Charlie,
        David,
            Jeffrey,
                and Danny.

Danny was the baby and therefore of no importance.
Jeffrey had a big head, like a potato. His brothers called him Big Head.
We called David "Daddy Longlegs."
  He was skinny as a straw, tall and giggly. When he grinned, you could see his chipped front tooth.
  You couldn't call him attractive, but he could kick the ball all the way across the street

high
a slow-
in motion
way arc
the that
all seemed
to stop time

Charlie was tall but jive—
    always looking past you,
    looking for something better on the horizon,
    always reminding you that you were just some white girl
    across the street, and he had bigger fish to fry.
George, the oldest, was handsome, polite, dependable. (A little boring, but nice.)

Mr. and Mrs. Lomack:
God-fearing, straight-laced souls.
I always smiled and called out "Hi, Mr. Lomack!" when I saw him.

These boys were the first boys I ever played with.
We played kickball together
on the triangular lot adjacent to our garage.
I always wanted to be on David's team,
because he could kick that ball all the way into Mrs. Simmons' yard.

I wasn't very good,
    barely bunting the ball no matter how hard I kicked,
But when dividing up for teams,
David never seemed to mind when I called out,
"I wanna be on David's team!"
He amiably allowed my sorry ass on his team without a protest.

Tolerant, quick, taking life in his long, long stride
bullet-headed, pistoling around the bases,
slapping me five if I made it to first…
David, which base did you eventually make it to?Did you ever reach home safely?
What are you doing?
I want to know. I'm afraid to know.

George could have gone into the army or the seminary. The
Reverend George W. Lomack. Sergeant Lomack.
Handsome in uniform. You always did like dressing up for
Sunday.
Charlie, if he's alive, has probably done time, dodged child
support payments, glanced over the accusatory gazes
of his children's mothers, said what they wanted to hear, slid
into stereotype.
Jeffrey, out of vengeance, must have gone into law or become a
stockbroker. Just to show them that this Big Head
had something in it.
Danny, I don't know.

But David.

What hope for David
scrawny as a beanpole with one cracked tooth and an easy grin?

Once you found a drawing in our trash can.
Mom had sketched my father's genitals,
in a moment of post-coital repose,
then tossed it away.
Days later, after that sketch had been fished out,
whooped over
and circulated among you and your brothers,
Mrs. Lomack greeted my mother in the street with a chilly,
"So *you* must be theartist'?"

Daddy Longlegs.
I thought it funny that a boy should
be called Daddy.

You were always more a greyhound than a spider
whippet thin—did you get enough to eat?—and fast.

You once chased away Carl Thornley,
mean freckled boy,
who sometimes beat me up.

As time passed,
I became the A student my parents
wanted me to be,
went to college and grad school,
got married, had kids.
I'd come home for visits and wave at you,
    the street now seeming like a vast divide.

What happened over the years?
Where are you now?
You, for whom the street had never been any big deal,
    just a canvas for your pretty arcs.
What widened that street

                                        wedged it into canyon?
Was it just awkwardness on my part, on yours?
Groping for small talk over the years, as kickball no longer
seemed to level the playing field.

Ok, George is still too perfect for words.
Jeffrey turned his anger into in-your-face success.
Charlie's a deadbeat dad, at best.
But not David.

Daddy Longlegs, this is my prayer for you.
I hope that you have
a secure job,
that you read the paper every day,
that you read to your children every night,
that you belong to a baseball league that meets on Saturdays
so that your kids can watch as you whip around the bases like nobody's business
and that someday
when you're sitting at your desk
after a long day of doing something boring but respectable
like adding receipts or filing ledgers or writing reports

you think back and remember this brown-haired girl
who always wanted
to be on your team

Centipede Morning

This morning at 5:09 a.m.
I waken to find another one in the tub.
I am transfixed by it.
I school myself to stare at it even when it runs.
I tell myself pieties that will make me feel more kindly towards it.

I cannot get on with my life until it is dead.
Until it is dead, the upstairs bathroom throbs
with potential danger, a hot zone.
If there is anything worse than a centipede in the tub
it's the sudden disappearance of that unkilled centipede, meaning
somewhere it lurks—in a wall, under a bureau, or (worse yet) up
the sleeve of a shirt
thrown carelessly down
that you might wear again.

Once, I put on a seemingly innocent plaid flannel shirt, sat in the car waiting for mom, then noticed the tail legs of one dripping from my pocket. It may have touched me. I ripped off the shirt, screaming, and then ran screaming, hopping, and slapping myself around and around the car until not only my mother came out but several of our neighbors. One old black man walking by was sure I had lost my mind. I could not get far enough from its faint whispery touch…

It is now 5:11 a.m. My husband sleeps, blissfully unaware
of the dilemma I face. I want to preserve his vegetable sleep, yet
I cannot leave my centipede
vigilance until it has been annihilated.
I accept the verdict:

It is a Jew, and I am a Nazi.
I tiptoe into the bedroom and whisper only,
    "There's one in the tub."
Twenty years has taught him to understand my ambiguous pronouns.
He grunts, "Oh," then groggily makes his way to the bathroom
while I retreat to the furthest possible corner of the upstairs. I
apologize to the sleeping bodies of my sons. When I return,
it is gone, and he is back in bed.

What is the source of my fear?
The legs—that rippling wave of movement, the speed, the stealth.
I want to gas not just six million but all of them.

Once, when my oldest son wailed
after my husband had killed one for me,
I drove to The Learning Shop
and purchased a plastic foot-long toy centipede,
in consolation. (*There's a market for these things?*)
I gave it to Zach, who slept with it.

I have tried.

Ken is asleep now. He has this gift:
he can sleep after killing,
his pulse steady.
He is my own private Gestapo,
my own killing machine.
I kiss his rough face in the dark.
My Adolph, my Hitler, my love.

Parable of the Vomiting Friend

Tia once threw up in our kitchen.
I must have been in first grade at the time,
so that would make her about four.

She never mentioned her food allergy—
that she was allergic to tomatoes,
so I poured us two glasses of tomato juice,
and showed her how I liked to put a little
tabasco sauce in mine—just a little.
We drank our juices like two men in a bar
having a Bud

except that she then got bug-eyed
opened her mouth
and started to upchuck tomato juice
all over the floor.

For me, this was Chernobyl—
a nuclear meltdown—
an outbreak of smallpox—
in my kitchen.

I screamed and ran out of the house
ran next door to get Tia's mother, Beverly.
It was very important to me
that Beverly be summoned immediately
as if only she—
    only she, mind you—
were equipped to clean up that small puddle of regurgitated tomato juice

now gracing our linoleum,
as if only she possessed the wisdom and
maybe one of those space-age, antiseptic, hazardous materials
suits that they have at the Center for Disease Control
to do the job.

I couldn't get rid of my friend quickly enough.
She had suddenly morphed into a
spewing fount,
a Weapon of Mass Destruction.

- - -

Some years later,
one New Year's eve,
Tia and I witnessed her brother's friend Brian Thomas
getting sick in their downstairs bathroom.
We watched from a safe distance
as her brother Evander and his other friend Terry Fellenz,
back from a night of drinking,
dealt with the situation.

Evander and Terry
stayed right beside Brian
in the bathroom,
holding his head, yelling for towels
    "Tia! Get me some towels! Hurry!"
                (she gingerly threw them to him,
                not wanted to enter the putrid zone)

Then they stripped off his soiled clothing.

Long, lean, yet muscular
was his coffee-colored torso.
("What a bod!" I thought, age 13.)

Limp, leaning on his friends,
and wearing only his white briefs,
like a loincloth,
he looked like Christ on the cross.

Vander and Terry half-carried
the limp figure upstairs, lay him in Vander's bed,
covered him up,
set up a wastebasket next to the bed
in case he had to heave again,
and then washed themselves up
prepared to go out
and party some more.

Tia and I watched this procedure
from a safe distance.

I was impressed by
their not running from him,
not cursing him
for his excesses or for interrupting
their evening.
No, they were efficient,
practical,
matter-of-fact.

I was most impressed
by Vander's installing this dormant Vesuvius
in his own bed.

Fast forward a decade.
I'm living on my own as a dorm counselor
in Milton, Massachusetts.
Ken and I eat spaghetti, drink red wine,
at his apartment, then go out for scorpion bowls
at a Chinese restaurant in Harvard Square.

Walking home, I find
          my knees buckle,
but we stagger home together,
          my buckly knees and I. And Ken.

Suddenly, my stomach   lurches
and I dash for the bathroom.

Inexperienced at efficient regurgitation,
nor one to frequent fraternity parties,
I begin disgorging my borrowed bits of spaghetti
into the bathroom sink.
Ken reached into the midst of the slop
to unclog and clean the sink.
I watched in awe.

I knew he was the one.

- - -

So that's what you do with a vomiting friend.
You don't vomit the vomiter.
You don't catapult him out of your house
as if he were some nameless, faceless criminal in a James Bond movie
haplessly sitting in the ejector seat.

Without flinching,
you hold his head,
you clean the mess,
you reach down into the middle of the muck,
if need be.
You place him in your own bed.
You digest him
    (every bitter ounce of him).
You wrap him
in a warm comforter,
preferably of flannel blue,
and let him sleep it off.

Scene from My Window

Lady Jane, stout cylinder
of bulldog,
sour, squashed face.
Wishbone, elegant greyhound,
retired from the race.

Elsie is not young.
She buried Will.
Her son is in another state.
This is her fate.

Elsie and Lady Jane
slowly wending
into view
as they always do.
Elsie with her puckish cap.
Lady Jane takes a crap.

Then it's Wishbone
for a stroll.
End of street,
a simple goal.

A quiet walk
for only two
will have to do.

Never Wishy running free—
Never Lady, off to pee—
Never Elsie, by herself—
leashes on a shelf.

The gentle clockwork of habit, trust
a life
devoid
of lust.

A Small Holocaust

"All my pretty ones?
Did you say all? O hell-kite! All?
What, all my pretty chickens and their dam
At one fell swoop?"
Macbeth IV, iii (216-219)

We took our boys to the Holocaust Memorial Museum
to introduce them
to World War II, Hitler, the rise of the Nazis, the death camps,
suffering.

Meanwhile,
a small holocaust
was awaiting us at home,
and grief needed no formal introduction.

All my pretty ones,
huddled together
stiff, cold, fur as lustrous as ever.
Waiting patiently for our return.

Three generations in one fell swoop.
Snore, gruff old grandmother, fat loaf of brown with a red rump.
Babushka providing childcare for your grandchildren,
huddling near the waiting two 'til the nursing two were done.
Phyllis, raven with a splash of coffee across your coat.
Friendly, outgoing, affectionate girl. You bore four babies but raised only your girl,
your boys sent off to Petco.
You shared what you had with your daughter,
tugging at your end of the lettuce leaf.

Calico Pie, timid beauty, sandwiched between grandmother and mother,
 sending your warning "brrr" at the slightest sound.
Three generations in one fell swoop.

Pretty chickens, why did you go?
Did you fear we'd never return?
Did you lose hope?
Did you perish of thirst? hunger? infection? heat?
Would gassing have been kinder?

The smell of death is sweet and sickly,
 like a note with a bent pitch.

My girls, you prove the better teachers
and what you teach is not to seek suffering
but to await it
for it will come
 in its own sweet time.

Elegy for Aunt Cleo

sips and
glimpses
sips and
glimpses

never got
to drink you up
rarely allowed
near the cup

'til the tannic
tea was old
til the cup
had grown
quite cold

though your shelf
was near my lips
all i got
were tiny sips

but you were still my cup of tea
beloved aunt, elusive she

Origins

I emerged from a stray copy of *The Worker's World, The Anarchist's Cookbook,*
three magic markers run out of ink,
one glue trap,
and my mother's kitchen cupboards with their jumbo boxes of elbow macaroni, swollen and rusty cans of pink salmon, dog biscuits for a long-dead dog.

I sprouted out of a few sprigs of wild spearmint,
growing into the side of the house,
a garage door of peeling white paint,
next to poison ivy vines and weed trees riotously uprooting the garage.
One trash can filled with bird seed.
A few ancient dog turds among the dandelions and crab grass.

I materialized at the intersection of Highways 33 and 35,
from a bin behind the Dunkin' Donuts across the street.
I'm from the abandoned Exxon Station, now just an empty lot with an orange fence around it.
Mom's home-made banner facing Highway 35 bellows:
"HELLO WAR IN IRAQ! GOODBYE SOCIAL SECURITY!"

I am from Takis and Dorothy, Mazzee and Bapa, Yaya, Aunt Andrea, Uncle Mickey, Aunt Cleo, cousins so numerous my sons cannot keep them straight.

I grew up hearing: "Nobody helps with the dishes. This house should be a commune, with everyone contributing"; "Men! I'm going to become a lesbian one day..."; "Amerika! I hate this country!"

I grew up hearing the quiet clack of billiard balls in the basement,
with dad's motto on the wall in chalk: "*Never hit the cue ball in anger.*
The cue ball will only do what you taught it."

I browsed among the bookshelves and found *Lolita*, *Moby Dick*,
Health Science, *The Medical-Legal Aspects of Death*.

I read *Little Women* until the pages began to shine with finger oil.

I grew up eating Mom's "meat testicles and spaghetti,"
her salads of iceberg lettuce and pale tomatoes,
her lunches of bologna slab sandwich, piece of fruit, and Raisinets;
Yaya's kiefthedes, her koulourakia,
her lamb with new potatoes and salata;
Mazzee's artful plates of hard-boiled egg and watercress,
her dishes of prunes in heavy cream, her carob bars and honey drops.
I choked down Bapa's bottomless bowls of raw turnip.

I deposit my memories for safe-keeping
in the cobbywebby memory of my mother (who invariably gets the facts wrong),
in the oft-repeated tales dragged out at family get-togethers
(the time Uncle Mickey swallowed a jar of aspirin and Mom got her post-coital clothes on faster than Dad, so she could drive Uncle Mickey to the emergency room, the time Cinnamon got lost at Allaire State Park and scolded us when we returned to fetch her),
in the many photo albums grouped unevenly in the basement,
and in this poem.

Anne of Cleves

Self-preserving soul
upstaged by her own portrait
disappointing in the flesh

But Anne was no idiot.
She took one look back at the fates of
wives 1 through 3
and decided to accept Henry's offer.

Three estates and financial independence for life
looked pretty good compared to alienation, decapitation, and death in childbirth.

Good-natured soul,
gave him a break,
an amiable divorce,
no need to contrive a new religion.
In relief and gratitude,
he gave her not one room of her own—
but three mansions-full,
honorary sisterhood to himself
and therefore a permanent place at court.
Also, her head's continued attachment
                                        to her neck.

Resigned to not getting a male heir from her,
after months of flaccid fumbling in the royal bedchamber,
Henry generously allowed the woman to
mother his neglected daughters,
   all so much flotsam and jetsam tossed overboard.

Anne with her cheery raft, raising a tea cup.
"Have another scone!"

No more boys for him but girls enough for the childless cast-away.

But when the court doctor publicized the fact of the king's nocturnal emissions
as a justification for divorce ("This marriage has not been consummated"),
publicized that the king had "selective" impotence
(couldn't get it up for Anne but already hankering for Katherine Howard),
then what…?

Then you wept a quiet weep, lovingly stroked the deeds to your estates, welcomed in the little princesses, urged
them to roast themselves before the fire in your best parlor,
and bustled off to ask the maid to set out the
Darjeeling and biscuits.

Elegy for Margaret Newlin

All these earnest young men.
I call them my bodyguards.

There must be at least three or four.

One or two are bald, one bearded. One tall.
They're all rather good-looking.
The bearded one reminds me of someone.

They ask me if there is anything I want
and tell me flattering tales about myself.
I'm a poet—quite good, they say—
I've written books of poetry!
Many books!
One even nominated for a National Book Award!
It's all very kind of them.
I smile to show my gratitude.
They mean well.

Why are they so kind? I sometimes wonder
what is it that they want from me?

I dream of the other place
with all the rooms,
each one rather fascinating
with its books and bric-a-brac and photos of
lovely children by the seaside.
The cats slinking about, rubbing up
against one's legs.

But one could easily get lost there.
I wandered often through those rooms.
Once I found my way to the kitchen,
where the dead fish floated on the surface
in their glass tank.
And then the dead kitties.
You found them everywhere.
So sad.

One of the earnest young men
appeared one day,
very serious,
    knitting his brow, talking on the phone.
Brought me to this room,
so I wouldn't get lost.

They always ask me what I would like, yet
it is they who seem so needy, so hungry for something,
some sort of assurance.
I smile often at them because they are so pleasant,
so accommodating, so well-spoken.

The bearded one sometimes weeps.
The bald ones are more restrained.
The tall one once grabbed my shoulders tightly and cried out,
"Jesus, Ma, don't you know me?! "
Really, I feared he might attack me.
Thank heavens the woman in the floral dress held him and drew him
    from the room.
He really seemed distraught.
I pitied him, felt embarrassed for him.
I obviously reminded the poor deluded soul of his deceased mother.

I have a whole host of words
somehow locked within an upstairs hall closet.
I cannot quite place the key,
but sometimes I feel a rich sense of possibility.

The bald one (John? Ron?) sometimes brings a young girl with him,
with curly brown hair and the loveliest blue eyes.
She reminds me of someone once dear to me.
She shows me drawings she has made of ballerinas
    and of an old woman and a little girl
                    in front of a large house.
Tapes them to the wall by my bed, in fact.
But I don't mind: children are always presumptuous.
Poor child thinks we are related, but
you can tell she only wants to be kind.
"We are all God's children," I console her.
But this only makes her sadder.

They're all so desperately needy.
Sometimes I grow impatient.
What do they want from me?

"Yes, I *would* like something," I snap at the tall one,
standing like a great oaf at my bedside,
interrupting my
bird-watching.
"Peace and quiet, if you must know!
No more damn sobbing men at the door."
He kisses me and leaves.

Most of the time, I am polite, though.
I smile sweetly and accept their gifts,
their photographs they are hellbent on showing me of
a petite, grey-haired woman
surrounded by a bevy of happy strangers.
I humor them and nod.

I can't think why they are so compelled
to intrude themselves, to enter
my room with their falsehoods and their photos,
their weepy eyes, their suffering patience.

I prefer to stare out the window
at the sturdy oak, struck by lightning,
to which a group of birds return
to make their nests
though the leaves are gone
and there's precious little shade.

Onion Soup

for Margaret Newlin

You once found a pink lima bean-
shaped newborn mouse,
which you nursed to maturity
using warm milk in an eyedropper.
You constructed a special habitat
in a separate room
in an enclosed area
with a heat lamp and soft material to burrow in,
mixing up nutritious mashes for
A. Nony Mouse.

Five cats roamed about your home.
I forget their names.
I do remember sitting down to tea and toast with you
and watching with interest
as a cat leaped up onto the dining table
and began serenely licking the stick of butter
in the butterdish.
Rested its haunches, made itself comfortable,
its tail swirling about.
No one budged or seemed surprised.
("No thank you, Mrs. N., I never take butter with my toast.")

The other thing I remember is the day
your youngest son got married.

He and I had once made onion soup in your kitchen.
He had baked some French bread.
I had brought a bottle of white wine in the shape of a fish.

I was cutting the onions and trying not to cry,
    as one invariably does while cutting onions.
We made a gallon of the soup, which we all sampled
    and pronounced delicious.

But I married another boy; your son, another girl.
On the day of his wedding, you turned to me
and said only, with one roguish eyebrow aloft,
"Onion soup?"

"Yes. Onion soup," I replied.

Kindred Spirits

I write down the title, "Four Lost English Teachers."
This stirs an immediate response.

Mr. Herbert points out that "lost" is not only imprecise and misleading but a euphemism of which George Orwell would not approve.

Mrs. Newlin mutters, "Elegy for Jane?" in that impish tone of hers.

Daria cocks her head to the side and point out that, strictly speaking, she had given up teaching
and had been editor-in-chief for *Commonweal* for some years now.

Cherie perks up at that. Another Catholic.

Let us take attendance:
Daria Donnelly: 43, editor of *Commonweal*, wife and mother of two small children
Margaret Newlin: 76, retired college professor, widow and mother of four grown sons
Dallas Herbert: 73, retired head of the English department at Neptune Sr. High School, never married, faithful caretaker of seven dogs
Cherie Castillo: 44, adjunct faculty at the University of Wisconsin—Fox Valley, mother of one son.

Our lives brushed up against one another.
We were cordial.

Daria I knew from graduate school: serious, scholarly, "our resident theologian," as one professor called her.

Mrs. Newlin the poetry-writing mother of a boy I knew in college. One of her books of poetry had been nominated for a National Book Award.
Mr. Herbert, exacting taskmaster, taught me 10th and 12th grade English.
Cherie, a colleague at Fox Valley, joined two book groups I organized. She ate little pretzels every day for lunch.

Now I introduce them. It's odd to yoke together folks from different areas of one's life. It feels like a wedding.

Mr. Herbert is gruff, uncommunicative, incapable of small talk. Daria sees that Cherie is uneasy and intimidated; they discuss their funerals, both in Catholic churches. Mrs. Newlin sees that she must take up the burden of initiating contact with her curmudgeonly contemporary and gamely asks him what book he last read, thinking all the while how much less handsome he is than her late husband.

"Before the hospital stay or in the hospital?" he asks, with unnecessary formality.

"Either," she smiles.

"I was re-reading *Middlemarch*, if you must know."

"Ah! You know what Woolf said of *Middlemarch* ? Something about its being the only novel written for adults."

Mr. Herbert grunts, lights a cigarette.

They won't ever make it to the discovery of their mutual love of animals, but they both smoke.

Daria is showing Cherie a photograph of her daughter, Jo, when suddenly Cherie turns to face me.

> "We're not 'lost,' Ellen. We're right here. And we know that we're dead. In fact, we're all mighty sick of all the euphemisms and cliches about fighting and struggling. Daria died of multiple myeloma—bad luck. Me, brain cancer. Again, bad luck. Margaret's 'complications due to Alzheimer's' is just a circuitous way of saying she walked out of her home half naked one day and froze to death under a tree. Dallas's heart stopped while he was having a dream about breaking up a dogfight." She sighs. It's like a gay man grown weary of having to come out of the closet to every newcomer he meets. So tiresome.

Daria has researched each of her new acquaintances and now turns to Mrs. Newlin, congratulating her for the National Book Award nomination. The two recogize each other's subtlety and confidence. Kindred spirits.

"Are you a poet too?" Mrs. Newlin asks.

"No, but I used to read a lot of poetry to my son, Ben. Longfellow. Whittier."

"Did you?!" Clearly delighted. The two begin reciting snatches of Longfellow. Mr. Herbert wants to join in.

Cherie has nothing to say to the pot-bellied older man until they spy a sign: "Everyone should remove their wet shoes."

Mr. Herbert looks at it, shakes his head, harrumphs.

Cherie gestures. "Don't you hate that? Even here there are agreement errors."

Mr. Herbert looks at her approvingly. "Lack of subject/antecedent agreement is one of my pet peeves, and you see this everyone/their formulation everywhere." His face choleric, he removes another cigarette.

"Did you teach high school English or were you an editor?" Cherie timidly asks.

He nods. "Both. I proofread for *The Asbury Park Press* and chaired the English department at a high school."

"What a coincidence! I taught remedial English at a two year college for over fifteen years."

It will take a few more centuries until Mrs. Newlin and Daria re-join the conversation.

Seized by Love

In memory of Britney and Brianna

A little boy wonders
why his mother seizes him
"C'mere, baby"
groaning and sobbing
and wetting his neck
with her tears and snot.

He wants to say
"I'm not a baby!"
but he senses
that it would be best
if he just said nothing.

His Legos sit there
in the corner,
his Matchbox cars
beckon.

Rocked like the baby he isn't,
he looks across the hall
to the locked door
of the nursery
that his father had just finished
painting
powder puff pink.

Now dad frowns and sighs
is on the phone all the time
talking about plots
"next to each other, that's right"
and pink satin lining
and mahogany.

"Why are you sad?"
the boy wants to ask,
but with a small child's infallible sense
of cause and effect,
he knows what that would get him:
a fresh gust of wailing
and rocking
and more tears and snot
down his neck.

Dadscapes

In memory of Takis Argyros, 10/12/76

September 11th was not my apocalypse.
October 12th was.

For me, you've been dead twice
as long as you've been alive.
The Venn diagram of our lives features two circles
overlapping by a scant fifteen years.

Three murky watercolor decades of you before my birth.

The first, an Edward Hopper scene—
streets of Newark
your father's candy store on a corner
the street fights.

The second, you a skinny 19 year old soldier
a Korean beauty on your arm in some club,
as you smoke nonchalantly,
all syphilitic charm and bravado.

The third, at Fitkin Hospital, where
you fought pneumonia in one room while I was bloodily emerging in another.
You survived, living to tell me your
bedtime stories of Eggen, the little girl who lived
in people's ears and ate earwax.

You brought me souvenirs from your visits to the city:
a purple paper Japanese fish that hung

from the ceiling, a papier-mache frog,
a colorful yarn snail.
You tested me on my lines,
teaching me the importance of always playing the villain
(you were Badri the Bandit, I the Wicked Witch).
You didn't trust the boys who lurked on the
outskirts of my womanhood.

Three decades of your absence
    a quiet, rolling cloud shadow
over all my rites of passage.

You were my age when your heart
had enough of the incessant pumping,
decided it needed a break,
fantasized about lazing in a Tahitian hammock
in the sun by a beach.
Left abruptly one morning without warning

left you groping for the nitroglycerin tablet,
which you jabbed under your tongue,
too late,
swerved the steering wheel
and pulled to the side of the road.

Thoughtful, really.
You didn't want t to take anyone with you.

Bratty Little Sister

It's not as if I was a classic bratty younger sister.
I was unorthodox in my methods.

Peed in a cereal bowl
carried hot sloshing urine
into her room
left it on her chair
giggling, huddled behind something, waited for her discovery
her indignant call to mom.

Pulled the shoelaces
out of each of her shoes
to tie the laces around the
handlebars of my tricycle.
Streamers. Cool.

Yelled, "MY SISTER LOVES YOU!!"
to the knock-kneed boy across the street,
seconds after she had confided
to me that he was in her chemistry
class.

Peered through a keyhole
at the boy lying on top of her
in her bedroom on the floor.
Their clothes on.
Too curious and mystified
to frame a sentence or
make a sound.

Secret Agent

For that slim decade when we lived together,
I sniffed and snooped and poked about my sister's things,
regarded them with curiosity and proprietary interest.

Things she brought home from school:
algebra books,
a compass
a set of cheerleading pompoms, red and black for Neptune Sr. High.
Little pep rally objects with cryptic messages like,
"Go Neptune! Swim the Waves!"
Also her lockable diary with its little key, hidden in her closet.
(A good incentive for me to learn to read.)

I pored over her tall, thin avocado Charm School book with its
pink whimsical fifties designs,
its impertinent questions about body types:
"Are you a stringbean? A dumpling? Or a princess?"
Its quaint suggestions about improving one's posture
by balancing an encyclopedia on one's head.

But she was eight years older than I
and therefore infallible.
I asked her which rocks were dinosaur eggs,
listening, rapt, to her answers.
She explained to me what menstruation was,
drew a diagram of a pear-shaped uterus.
She took me to get my first fitted bra.
Left behind her records—"Secret Agent Man,"
"Red Rubber Ball," "The Bloody Red Baron"—
the soundtracks of my youth.

Some of what she taught me was unintentional.

I watched her fight with mom
over clothes, over money.
I watched her marry at twenty,
move across the country,
rarely come home.

I quietly absorbed
every lesson
with the attentiveness and stealth of a
secret agent
sneaking back down
the alley
with my stolen
goods, the
contraband
of childhood.

The Wanted Child

i.

The zygote is a tiny little seed
Of blood and pulse and nervous system new.
One nurtures it according to one's need.
The wanted babe is far between and few.
The wanted babe is fed protein and milk.
Its every move is chronicled and noted.
Its future crib festooned with softest silk.
Upon its life, its proud parents have doted.
Unwanted babes feel very much like tumors
that cause one to grow ever pale and queasy.
They swell one's belly, causing nasty rumors.
Removing them? It should be quick and easy.
If pity for desp'rate lasses is begrudged,
Then sin ye not, lest you yourself be judged.

ii.

But *my* pity is for th' unwanted ones—
The she's routinely tossed away in China.
Their only crime? Not to have been born sons,
But bearers of the second-rate vagina.
These tiny girls ne'er asked to be conceived
Or to be thrown on rubbish heaps of dung
Though of their mis'rable lives they'd be relieved
if in piranhas' pools instead were flung.
The heroes in my world are those like Mia
Who take these little girls into their hearts,
whether they hale from China or Korea.
Adoptive parents offer babes new starts.
If "orphan or abortion" is the choice,
Then let us choose adoption with one voice.

iii.

Adoption is a happy accident.
"Infertile couple meets with healthy child."
Statistically, these folks are heaven sent;
Rejected children often turn out wild.
Of China's fifteen million throwaways,
The slend'rest fraction will find happy homes.
The others will spend countless wretched days
Deprived of food and love and warmth and poems.
So let us be clear-eyed about adoption.
It is the morally superior choice.
For many, though, it's not even an option
Instead of one, let's speak in many a voice.
Let's speak instead of ready birth control,
A worthy and a useful global goal.

While Reading on the Cell Cycle, I Find a Poem

"The cell rounds up
and loses contact with its neighbors."
(*When you left, I gained 30 lbs., stopped
walking with Linda, did not participate in Chris's
garage sale, and stopped attending my book club.*)

"The nucleus fragments, and the plasma membrane develops blisters."
(*I could not concentrate on any project. I forgot to pick up the boys
from their football practices, and the dog started shitting in the house
again. Blisters, eczema, constipation—you name it. I had it.*)

"Finally the cell fragments…"
(*I could not continue to make the mortgage payments, so we had to move
to West Roxbury. The boys had to adjust to a new school system where they
were beaten up regularly after school. I gained another 20 lbs., and my
cholestrol went through the roof.*)

"…and its bits and pieces are engulfed by white blood cells and/
or neighboring cells."
(*At the moving sale, Chris purchased the crystal decanter given to us as a
wedding present by one of your parents' friends. Rena's children purchased the
boys' old Lego sets and their Playskool pirate ship and castle. Kevin bought
all your power tools that you left behind.*)

"Cells routinely harbor the enzymes that bring about apoptosis."
(*And I got very friendly with Jack Daniels.*)

The Dragonfly

Something landed on my leg.
It was a dragonfly.

not elegant with iridescent wings
or spots of unearthly blue tipped with black

it was an adolescent dragonfly—
shades of gray and clear
with black dots on its eye buds
and stripes of black on its long thorax

its wings were folded together,
gummed at the ends with a drop of yellowish goo

How to disentangle its wings?
I found a blade of grass and inserted it
    between the wings of the dragonfly.
This helped remove the drop of goo,
    but the wings had been crushed together in an unnatural way
that interfered with its ability to fly

Every now and then, it would raise its thorax, lift its oddly folded wings, flutter them, and then settle back down into a kind of resignation.

So unlike human adolescents,
the creature was cooperative, open to suggestion,
    it cheerfully tiptoed onto my finger
It would move from one finger to another quite amicably,
    making no resistance,
trusting the moving walkway.

I brought it over to the sandbox,
    where my sons were now playing with some other children.
They stopped momentarily to look at it,
but did not want to build it a special house out of sand.

> (They were noisy. There were eight children in the sandbox. I had to speak harshly when two of them started to throw sand at one another.)

I carried the dragonfly to safer ground, near a bench.
There, I speculated on how to insert the grass in such a way as to help it fly.
Short of ironing its queerly folded wings,
there was little that could be done for it.
Again, it would flutter, as if to attempt flight,
but such fluttering seemed more and more futile and pathetic.

I carried it into the house and held it for two hours,
Letting it amble from hand to hand.
Finally, tiring of it
and wanting to reclaim my hands and make dinner,
I let it go

Moth at 5 a.m.

One morning at 5 a.m.,
having just spent an all nighter
working on a chapter of my paper on the maturation of the self in Proust and Wordsworth
I was sitting at my desk...
my hands poised on the keys of the typewriter.

My mind had gone blank.
I couldn't think of what to write.

No one else was awake in the dorm.
Naked couples lay sleeping in one another's arms,
    hoping the condom didn't break.
Drunken lads and lasses, having returned from carousing at 2 a.m.,
    heavily weighed down in exhausted slumber and dried vomit.
I heard no crashing bathroom door, no whispered voices,
    no telephone ring, no car doors, nothing.

I was on Mars
or a vacant, lunar landscape.

As I sat there,
I suddenly became aware of a
delicate touch of my right pinky.

A moth had lit upon it,
settled there.
A plain pale beige specimen.
I stared down at the moth perched on
my motionless pinky.

It stayed there,
comfortable.
I was its chair.
It was my company.

It required my stillness.
I was delighted by this small sign of life
that had chosen me
for its perch.

In deference to its trust,
and wanting to be a really good chair,
I did not move
for a long time.

Millipede

a shiny, black millipede
on a picnic table outside at the Children's Museum in Boston

It had so many legs that it made me shiver.
They rippled as it slithered noiselessly across the table.

Finally, I summoned up the nerve to pet it.
I wouldn't touch the wriggling legs,
just the black exoskeleton
shiny and hard like an acorn.

When I touched it, it curled up
into a   tightlittleball,
and lay still,
pretending to be dead.

It was not impressed by my attempt to desensitize myself,
to exorcise my schkeeves,
to express affection for it.
It was frightened.
It feared I would squish it or eat it or carry it in my talons to feed it to my young.

I thought of the time Carl Thornley
across the street beat me up,
            I too had curled up into a ball,
            protecting my head and ears,
making myself as tiny as possible
making myself invisible.

The millipede lay there coiled, motionless, a black fiddlehead.

I stopped petting it
and watched as it gradually uncoiled itself,
          relaxed and began its
                    solemn business of slithering slithering slithering
                    across the table…

Graveyard

This graveyard's such a solitary place:
An urn, a mausoleum, and a vase.
All capitals, a name like JONES.
A square tomb over sedentary bones.
A spire uplifted, pointed at the sky
inspires me to wonder how I'll die.
This place of rest retains no trace of humor
Or lust or rage or giggling huddled rumor.
Did not the recent dead know how to smile?
Or flirt or fart or strut their stuff in style?
I want to see more traces here of life—
Of sweaty, laughing, panting man and wife.

The Red Efts of Ganoga Lake

The red efts of Ganoga Lake
surface only after a rain.
Crawl through grasses, sedges, hay-scented fern.
Lie hidden under fossilized shale, emerging into the moisture.

Ill-named. More orange than red.
A bright pumpkin color with dots of red.
Beautiful but toxic, indigestible,
they suffer the indignity of being
tasted and spat out
by would-be predators.

Snake saliva, coyote saliva,
huge Goodyear whitewall tires like tanks
barrelling down the road after a rain.
These are their enemies, as are little boys
with terraria.

Red eft! Run across my hand.
Gentle rubbery touch as I transfer you
from hand to hand,
floor to floor.
So trusting, vulnerable, fey.
Eft, soon you will become the elusive salamander—
black, secret, swimming in dark water,
Rarely seen.

But for now you are mine
moisture-loving road-farer
lovely to see
soft to touch
death to taste.

Old Haunts

When I was a child,
there were places
where I felt welcome

Yaya's apartment—with its sunbeams of dust flecks and green satin ribbons tied to her plants,
reading *Pogo* while leaning against a hot radiator at Mazzee's house,
Saturdays in the summer at Diane's tiny house in Spring Lake Heights, floating in her pool,
walking downstairs at the Asbury Park Public Library to the children's section and finding
    Wally the Word Worm, *The Tall Book of Make-Believe*, the hiding places book with the orange and
    pink striped cover
visits to Allaire State Park with its Deserted Village, walking trails, and penny candy
dinners with my parents' friends, Jean and Al, reading *Reader's Digests* in their bathroom
Uncle Mickey's small apartment—easels and paintings, stink of linseed oil
Charlie's unkempt bachelor quarters, reek of machinery grease, his unmade bed, and a pint of buttermilk
    drunk from the carton
tea and koulourakia with Anna Boyitges, in her immaculate living room

Each dwelling,
an immersion

Some places, let's face it, were unbearable.

The Kemmlers' home with graffiti on the walls and nothing but a can of cream soup to eat. I couldn't
    stay there even one night.
One uncle, pricked by an old quarrel, snarled at me. I ran and never looked back.
Some houses reek of cat litter boxes and hoarding and madness.

But some places nourish you just to think of them.
Aunt Andrea effortlessly preparing spreads of spanikopita, salata, pastitsio, kourambiethes, baklava.
    She kept a running conversation going, as she sliced cucumber.
    I remember the back of her, as she worked in her kitchen.
With Diane, in her two piece bathing suit, it was gin and tonics, sliced pepperoni, cheddar, Ritz crackers.
Mazzee made you identify all the veggies in her homemade soup.
Her kitchen fragrant with ripe pears,
    golden apples, watercress, and her candy drawer full of honey drops, carob, and sesame seed bars.

When you lose the person,
    you lose the place as well.

You stand outside Yaya's old house, with its new beige siding, chain link fence, and smells of fried food.
You stand outside where you think Diane's house used to be, luxury condos in its stead.
Anna's house has been repainted,
    someone behind the venetian blind eyes you suspiciously, one hand on the phone

You stand outside your favorite haunts,
                    no longer welcome.
This is what it means to grow old.

I miss Yaya
but so much of what I miss about her is
inseparable from
where she lived
I miss her apartment too,
like an old friend
buried long ago
without my noticing

He's Got Mail

Every genocide
marks a holiday.
God taking a break.
Not checking in with the office.
Not turning on His cell phone.
Leaving His laptop behind.

Prayers left unanswered
    will eventually be heard
after His luggage is found,
laundry done,
plants watered,
pets back from the kennel,
mail service and newspaper subscriptions
    re-activated.

He's always a little frumpy and jet-lagged
after a few weeks or months or years
elsewhere
on some sunny tropical isle
in another galaxy.

After the Holocaust, Nuremberg.
He'll get around to it.

Darfur Lullaby

Every tedious genocide
Means God has taken a little ride.
He's passed over to the other side
To thin the herd a bit.

The planet's equilibrium
Is kept in check by watchful Him.
And though it seems he leaves on whim
He's cleverer than that.

Young men are killed, their sisters raped,
No Superman arrives, encaped,
And none of the innocent escaped.
But God is getting a tan.

When He returns, He collects the post
(for the Father, Son, and the Holy Ghost),
listens to voice mail, esp. the most
beseeching, and ignores the rest.

If we're in God's image, we deserve what we're getting,
a little herd-thinning, a little blood-letting,
and God deserves his bit of jet-setting
and letting us fend for ourselves.

So pray, pray, pray if it makes you happy
But God's not your servant—he won't be snappy
(and sometimes his service is downright crappy).
Take care of it yourself.

Gesture Drawing

My mother is a banner proclaiming,
    NO BLOOD FOR OIL
She is a yellow steno pad of Gregg shorthand,
notes taken at a town meeting.
A stack of flyers,
a set of car keys (lost).

She is a bevy of bumperstickers
competing for space
on the rear of her car.
"Impeach Bush."
"Stop Eminent Domain Abuse."

She is sometimes a horror movie,
The Ring, The Omen, The Shining,
though she's more often *Burn* or *JFK* or
Sicko.

Every Saturday, after picketing, she is a $5.99 All You Can Eat buffet
at the Imperial Garden.
Kung Pao chicken, sauteed snow peas, red jello.

She prides herself on being a good bargain,
an elegant, designer-made piece at a
rock bottom price.
She's always been off the rack,
ready to wear.

She is the scourge
of local politicians,

a Fury
at the dais.

Every day she is a brisk constitutional through
Monmouth Mall with her friend
and the other mall-walkers,
though sometimes she is a walk through
Palaia Park instead, if the weather is fine.

If a friend is going through a bad time,
my mom is a frantic car ride, a long conversation,
vigilant concern.

She can also be a chuckle and a smutty joke,
told twice
during the same phone call.
"Stop me if I told you this…"

And once a week she is a sketchpad
and a set of charcoals
and the graceful lines of a nude model,
a gesture drawing.

Memory of a Texture

It's a frigid February
afternoon,
late sun, long shadows

the snow dryly crunches,
stiffly resistant
like styrofoam

and it's been a long time
since I've thought of
styrofoam

and of the time, forty years ago,
when Linda Jane Kemmler and I prowled around in our attic—
everything strewn about,
because squirrels had gotten in,
looking for nest material

Linda and I,
foraging too,
found a
solar system

my sister's school project
long since discarded
up among the loose insulation
and the mouse turds,
the broken Christmas ornaments,
mustard gold jodhpurs
and riding crop

each planet colored
with fluorescent
magic marker

Optimistically,
I took a bite out of
the cheery yellow sun.
Linda tried one
of the gas planets,
Jupiter (with its cherry red spot)

our teeth meeting in the
stiff, crisp, brittle
middles

We spat out the sun and Jupiter
but readily ingested that tired platitude,
appearances sometimes deceive.

Cold Potato Boy

In memory of Emmett Till

The toddlers in the courtroom were bored,
as fidgety children are when held captive in church.
Their fathers were on trial for murdering a boy
they'd never know, the only child of Mamie Till.
Blonde toddlers in starched shirts squirmed on indulgent papa laps,
conspicuous advertisements of their fathers' love.

The bloated white potato face of a boy once loved
by a shell-shocked mother, now bears a hole that a bullet bored
through his skull moments after he remembered the warm laps
of his parents years ago in a North Chicago church
where his father, in uniform, gently hushed him. A happy child 'til
he whistled at that white woman. The bravado of a boy

only fourteen years old, an age when any boy
pretends that he is cool, brave, impervious to fear or love,
eager to impress his yokel cousins with his worldly ways 'til
the white woman's tale of having been whistled at bore
like a screwdriver in the brain of her husband sitting in church
doing a slow burn, contemplating a brutal lapse

in what little humanity he possessed, running laps
in the marathon of tortures he might inflict upon the boy
though the man was an active participant in his church
and sang in a rich alto voice of Jesus's love,
taking restless Jasper to the potty, lest he get bored,
sometimes dipping his hand into the till

and often letting the sermon wash over him until
the end, glad-handing fellow parishioners, quite content, but with a lapse
of sympathy when it came to other people's sons, using a board
and an iron weight to hold down the buoyant corpse of the boy
his mother—loathe to let her child go south—so loved
and laid to rest, with heaving sobs, in the crowded church.

How odd that homicidal fathers sit, too, in church
or courtrooms, festooned with their blond babies, 'til
Jet showed the world the face of the cold potato boy. The love
and outrage of a nation swarmed around Mamie, whose life would lapse
into despair. "Let the people see what they did to my boy."
She would insist on an open casket. The bulletin board

proclaimed a pot luck and the miracle of God's love. The track team would run laps
around the helpless preacher in his church until
the cold potato boy was laid to rest, his skull a bullet board.

Greece with Kids

At the Acropolis,
in the blazing sun,
the boys are wilting.

Zach hunches up in a ball
arranges piles of stones into little men.

Max, wandering, makes a friend,
a Greek boy who spots him
and calls out *"Hey boy!"*
The two smash rocks and
shells and play together,
wordlessly,
sometimes blurting out random things
in their mother tongues.

Since I am trailing Max,
I don't get to hear much
of what our tour guide is
saying about the Acropolis.
A few words about Pericles
drift through…

We spend a whole day
in Rhodes and tour
the Palace of the
Grandmaster.
The boys befriend
two dogs,
lolling in the shade.

At the hotel in Mytilene,
Max meets two cats.
Zach, on his Gameboy, reaches the Elite Four.
We subsist on a box of
HoneyNut Cheerios
until lunch is available
at the taverna next door,
not until 1 p.m.
at the earliest.

My cousin's wife, Voula, asks
Zach and Max
if they want to play with
her grown sons'
Sony Play Station.
While they play,
Aryeris and Maroula
sit next to them,
stroke their hair,
and talk to them.
Max asks the next day:
"Are we going to see
Maroula and Aryeris today?"
They are all he will remember about this trip.
(They and the stray dogs.)

Portrait of Uncle Mickey

You were a room with three easels
the smell of linseed oil, bright and pungent,
palettes smeared with ochre, gold, bloodred, raw umber,
postcards of Picasso's "Three Musicians"
wedged in mirrors.

You were a pulmonary embolism,
a sixpack of schizophrenia,
a closet, locked and private.

Your pupils darted nervously.

You were a fascination with Braque,
Picasso, Cubism.
Yours was a thick line, a jigsaw design,
a jerking of perspective.

You were a clipper ship
in red and gold and white and brown
or maybe it was laundry on a line between
two tenements

You were a man seated on a donkey
in a pale yellow and lavender wildnerness
of rocks and canyons.

You were a lithograph
of three black men being lynched,
their bodies shining
with defiance.

You were and always will be
the gift of a Hershey's chocolate bar
rare, delicious, and gone too soon.

Stranger at the Door

You would occasionally drop by,
ring the bell.
I'd peer out the peep hole
and spy
a wild, shaggy stranger
in a leather jacket,
stamping out a cigarette on our top step.
Lean and dangerous.

I'd debate whether to open the door.

Reluctantly,
I'd open it a crack.
"May I help you?" I'd say in my receptionist's voice.
"Is Uncle Tacky home?" you'd ask.

Uncle?

It would take me a few moments
to deduce who you were,
to discern that we were kin,
shared a gene pool.
You weren't Caliban; I wasn't Miranda.
It was ok.

"Oh!" I would swing the door wide.
I'd had a crush on you for many years,
back when you were your mother's son
and looked, well, civilized.

I'd let you in and call out
to my father playing pool
in the basement,
"Dad! Cousin Gregory's here!"

My father, happy to see his sister-son,
wastrel of the streets, echo of himself,
would take you downstairs
to our grimy basement
of pool sticks, cues,
ivory balls in rich hues of violet, royal blue, kelly green, fire engine red, bright orange and yellow,
little blue cubes of chalk, baby powder,
and dad's regulation size pool table, its leather pockets, its taut green sheet of flannel.

I could gain access
by playing the hostess,
carry down a tray with glasses
of juice, ice cubes clinking.
I'd hang around,
listen to what men talked about.
Shyly ask you questions.

"How is Jean?"
Fond memories of a leggy blonde
with large green eyes.
Athena said you used to carry Jean into the attic,
your parents, unsuspicious, hearing only
one set of footsteps.
Once up there, you'd do
forbidden things.

You teased me when I was very young,
thought me a hot house flower,
bullied me, made me cry.
My mother once yanked you by the ear
and locked you outside our front door,
your own mother rooting her on.

But then you mellowed
and I grew up
and liked to sit on your lap,
my handsome, tan, gentle cuz,
vaguely resembling Cat Stevens,
my idol.

You were twenty
when we got the phone call.
A car accident.
A coma.

It was June of 1977.
Everyone had died the previous year,
Uncle Mickey, Dad, Yaya.
I figured the family quota
had been met.

And you were twenty.

"Let's wait until he's out of his coma
to see him," I suggested to Mom.

Because you were twenty
and dangerous
and therefore, I reasoned,
you couldn't die because
you'd frighten Death,
make him want to deadbolt his door and pretend to be not home.

But you didn't.

Aunt Andrea's face
fell into a mask of sadness.
Priests with somber faces
drove down from Newark and Hazlet.
Hundreds of teens attended your funeral.
(I buried a silver and turquoise ring
with you. My own small offering.)

You've been gone for thirty years now.
Uncle Tacky is gone.
The pool table, gone.
The house, gone.
Your girl Jean is married and a grandmother.

Baby College

I attended Baby College,
without knowing it,
in 1990
on Warwick Road.

Ours was a condo association of
three floors, each with its resident swollen belly.

Top floor, last to go: I pushed out Zach in early fall.
Second floor, first to go: Christine gave birth to Matthew in winter.
First floor, second to go: Franny bore Rosalynn in late spring.

As last one in line, I bore
the full brunt of everyone's best wishes and unsolicited advice.

Happy notes on the downstairs notepad
in the vestibule near the mailboxes.
"Congratulations! We are so thrilled! Welcome, Baby Zach!"

Christine already had Jennie,
so she was a pro.
Took control of Matthew's circadian rhythm
like a seasoned ranch hand with a lasso:
spanged the baby's feet to keep him awake all day.
Took one week of this to get him to sleep through the night.
She always looked freshly showered, pink-cheeked,
wearing matching clothes and make-up.

All I did was breastfeed
and sleep.

Wear pajamas all day,
my hair matted with milk.

Franny was as inexperienced as I was,
despite her wall of childcare books.
Her place a fertile mess of funky playthings
and books with titles like *Massaging Your Newborn*,
Serenading Your Baby In Utero.

We shared stories of our mutual
cluelessness.
I remember her shock at the seam of crud.
(Apparently, one has to separate
the labial lips in order to clean
one's baby girl properly.)

Sometimes she enjoyed playing the teacher.
She called me up one day when I was
near the end of my third trimester to say,
"I'm about to give Rosalynn a bath.
Wanna come watch?"

Another day I watched as Franny
tied the bib on and then fed
Rosalynn a mash of tofu, strained squash,
peas, and carrots.
In it all went.
"That's probably extremely healthy," I thought.

In a year or two,
Christine, Dick, Jennie, and Matthew would be moving into
a new home.

I knew it would be spanking clean,
nicely decorated,
in a neighborhood with other children.

A few years later, Franny, Bill, and Rosalynn moved to a house in
a community of like-minded folks.
Not quite a commune, but with
communal areas for play and gatherings.
An organic garden.

Eventually, we would move with our Zach
to Wisconsin and a neighbhorhood with
twenty-six children in a one block radius.

But for that first year of Zach's life,
I was lucky enough
to attend Baby College,
with its research inquiries
(circumcision or not?),
its seminars
(cloth or disposable?),
its politics
(breast or bottle?),
and its many,
          many,
             many all-nighters.